Love-Based Copywriting Method:

THE PHILOSOPHY BEHIND WRITING COPY THAT ATTRACTS, INSPIRES AND INVITES

by Michele PW (Michele Pariza Wacek)

This book may be purchased for educational, business, or sales promotional use. For information, please email info@michelepw.com.

ISBN 978-0-9968260-1-3

Library of Congress Control Number: 2015917777

DEDICATION

I want to thank Nancy Marmolejo, Amethyst Wyldfyre and all the other conscious entrepreneurs who saw the vision of this book before I did (not to mention held my feet to the fire until I actually lived up to that vision).

Susan Liddy for giving me Love-Based — which was the final puzzle piece that allowed everything else to fall into place.

Christine Arylo for being my spiritual mentor and helping me clear the crap out of my head so I could finally start to truly come from love and abundance.

Andrea J. Lee for being my writer buddy and helping me stand into my vision.

Megan Yakovich for her wise and heartfelt editing.

Karin Wilson and Erin Ferree Stratton for providing the beautiful, visual design to bring these books into life.

And Paul for his love and support.

xxoo

CONTENTS

Foreword

BY SUSAN LIDDY, FOUNDER OF THE LOVE-BASED BUSINESS PARADIGM MOVEMENT

As a consumer, I always hated marketing and advertising.

I hated how they triggered my fears, made me feel less than incapable and tried to manipulate me into the sale.

So, of course, one of the first things I noticed when I entered the business world as a business owner was how much fear was rooted in the coaching industry. Pretty much all the marketing, sales and copywriting was fear-based.

The last thing I wanted to do was dump more fear-based marketing messages into the world, so I started to search for a better way. Unfortunately, all I found were "gurus" who were actively teaching and encouraging the use of the tactics that I deplored.

At first I despaired. Until I realized I was the one who was meant to step up and be that expert in the Love-Based Business Paradigm.

As time went on, though, I've come to realize an even deeper message. I see now that while I was meant to give birth to the Love-Based Business Paradigm, I was not meant to nurture and grow it by myself. The Love-Based Business Paradigm

1

needs a bigger platform than what I can do by myself as an entrepreneur.

It needs to be a movement.

They say that it takes a village to raise a child, and it most certainly takes a village to raise a movement. To honor that, I invite all coaches and service-based business owners to use their version of Love-Based Business and spread the movement far and wide. Together, we can change how marketing and advertising is being done.

Michele PW is a gifted copywriter who knows and understands love-based copywriting inside and out. She has done incredible work for me and my business and I am honored that she is taking the lead in bringing love-based copywriting front and center with this book that you now hold in your hands.

With all my love.

Susan Liddy

Author of "Love-Based Marketing: The No Sell-Out, Copy-Out, Burn-Out Method to Attract Your Soul Mate Clients into Your Business" www.SusanLiddy.com

Introduction
WHY THIS BOOK?

I've wanted to write this book for a good long time, even if I didn't fully realize it until recently.

As a child (3 years old), I taught myself to read because I wanted to write stories so badly.

As a teenager, I tried to figure out what to do to make money while I wrote my novels. Everyone said I should be a journalist, but that was the last thing I wanted to be.

Instead, while in college, I discovered the wonderful world of copywriting.

Copywriting, which has nothing to do with protecting intellectual property or putting a copyright on something, is all about writing promotional materials for businesses. Businesses have a lot of copy they need written, but rather than hire a lot of employees to get it all done, they use freelancers. Hence, there's an entire freelance copywriting industry out there devoted to serving those businesses.

For years, I bounced between freelancing and working full time (which included freelancing as I was working) until 1998 when I quit my job to pursue full-time copywriting.

Along the way, I discovered I had a talent for not only writing promotional copy, but also for crafting marketing strategy. I also discovered I was most passionate and excited when I was working on campaigns that directly resulted in my clients growing their businesses. Put those two together, and it made sense for me to stop being a generic copywriter who would write anything (and as a side note, being a generalist is NOT a great business model) and instead specialize in direct response copy and marketing.

Direct response copy is actually a subset of copywriting. It's a specialized form of writing copy where folks are directly responding to the marketing piece by taking action. That action could be anything from clicking a link in an email to exchanging a name and email for access to a training call to buying a product. (Other examples of traditional direct response include infomercials and junk mail — and if you're like most folks, the term "junk mail" doesn't evoke fuzzy hearts and rainbows type feelings. Traditional direct response copy like this HAS gotten a bad rap - more to come on this, below.)

Because direct response copy does a lot of heavy lifting for the business owner or entrepreneur, it's actually an extremely powerful tool to have in your toolbox. When you master this skill, you have the power to simply send an email and watch sales come in.

So, it sounds like a no-brainer to use direct response copy in your business. Right?

Well…

Have you ever been reading an online sales letter, and as you scroll down looking for the price (all the while wondering if anyone actually reads these things), you can't help but feel like the copy is hype-y, sales-y, and inauthentic?

If you're an entrepreneur or a business owner, have you ever consequently cringed at the thought of using direct response copy in your own business?

These feelings are likely amplified if you consider yourself "conscious" or "heart-centered" or "spiritual" or "transformational" or "creative." You may even feel completely out of integrity at the thought of using a tool in your business that feels so inauthentic.

Worse, if you've ever tried to tell the "gurus" how you don't want to use direct response copy because of how it makes you feel when you read it – that you want an alternative - you may have basically been told to quit bellyaching and pull up your "big girl" or "big boy" panties. After all, you WANT to make money from your marketing materials, don't you?

I know this happens, because a lot of my friends and clients in the transformational industry have experienced it. That's why they encouraged me to come up with a new way to write copy that didn't feel so "icky." They proposed names like "conscious" copywriting or "attraction" copywriting, but that didn't feel right to me. I didn't necessarily want to create an alternative way to write copy (which could be considered "less than" traditional direct response copywriting — "if you're not a REAL business owner, you can go use that attraction copywriting, but if you're serious about your business, you'll buckle down and use grown-up direct response copywriting").

What I wanted to do was transform the entire direct response copywriting industry. I just didn't know how.

And then my friend Susan Liddy came into my life (you can read more about her in the Foreword, if you haven't already).

Susan wrote a book titled "Love-Based Marketing: The No Sell-Out, Copy-Out, Burn-Out Method to Attract Your Soul Mate Clients into Your Business." Basically, she wanted to offer an alternative to marketing that was based in love, rather than fear.

Hmmm.

That's when it hit me: could this be what was happening with that "icky-feeling" copywriting, too?

Is traditional copywriting based in fear?

And then the epiphany: what if we wrote copy based in love?

Love-based copywriting.

That's when all the pieces fell into place.

I published my first Love-Based Copywriting book in August, 2014. I called it "Love-Based Copywriting: How to Write Copy That Attracts, Inspires and Invites Your Ideal Prospects to Become Ideal Clients." And it was a huge hit.

I had entrepreneurs reach out to me everywhere in the world to tell me how this book completely transformed their business. It gave them a sense of peace that nothing else ever had.

So my mission was clear. I needed to get the word out about love-based copywriting.

I spent a year promoting it — writing articles, blog posts and getting on dozens of radio shows, podcasts and live stages to spread the word. And along the way, I became even clearer about what love-based copy is, and the philosophy behind it.

And somewhere along the way, I realized that first book needed an upgrade. There was more I needed to say about the philosophy behind writing love-based copy.

With the new edition came a new title, too — "Love-Based Copywriting Method: The Philosophy Behind Writing Copy

That Attracts, Inspires and Invites" (which is the book you now hold in your hand).

(Another side note here — sometimes getting your work out there, even if you later realize it's not as perfect as it could be, is the best thing you can do. Only by talking about the book to other people and getting their feedback and questions was I able to see what I needed to do to make the book stronger.)

I also realized I needed a second Love-Based Copywriting book, which would focus more on the "how-to" when it comes to writing love-based copy. It needed to teach all the specific nuts and bolts involved, such as writing headlines, features and benefits and more.

So, I also wrote a second book — "Love-Based Copywriting System: A Step-by-Step Process to Master Writing Copy That Attracts, Inspires and Invites."

While the two books are magic together, they also stand well on their own.

So, if you are looking to learn the philosophy around writing love-based copy, including how to emotionally connect with your ideal clients using psychological triggers (or hot buttons) in a love-based way, this book is for you. It doesn't matter if you're a beginner or advanced entrepreneur; if being love-based in your copy and/or marketing is important to you, this book can help you accomplish that.

If you're interested in writing your own love-based copy, after reading this one about the philosophy behind it, then my "Love-Based Copywriting System" is also for you. (You can learn more here: www.LoveBasedCopyBooks.com.)

Love-Based Copywriting Method:

How to Use This Book

Even though this book doesn't get into the nuts and bolts of actually writing copy, you'll still find a lot of exercises and strategies to help you integrate the love-based philosophy into your marketing and copy.

I start by describing the basics, so you get the foundation - the love-based copy principles. Once you have a clear understanding of what love-based copy is (and how it compares to fear-based), then I move into exercises, so you can start implementing those principles into your business.

In the Resources section, I provide additional supporting materials plus next steps, depending on where you are in your business and where you want to go next.

And, if at any time, you decide the last thing you want to do is write your own copy, we'd love to do it for you. You can learn more about our services at www.MichelePW.com/services.

Love-Based Copywriting Method:

Chapter 1
WHAT IS LOVE-BASED COPY?

Before you can fully understand the concept of love-based copy, you need to clearly understand direct response copywriting.

There are actually 2 things to consider here.

On the surface, direct response copy is writing promotional materials that get people to take action — to directly respond to the written material. (Remember, this has nothing to do with putting a copyright on something or protecting your intellectual property.)

But what direct response copywriting REALLY is, above all else, is leverage and freedom. Good direct response copy will do a lot of the heavy lifting for you – that's the leverage part. It will allow you to market and sell one-to-many versus one-to-one.

You see, if you aren't using direct response marketing and copy in your biz, then chances are your sales and marketing activities look something like this:

- 💜 You go out and hustle up some prospects by networking (online or offline) and talking to folks.

- 💜 You follow up with them one-on-one, with calls and emails.

- ♥ You meet with them again, and have a sales conversation.

- ♥ You personally continue to follow up with them (again and again) until they say either "yes" or "no."

Now, when you use direct response copy in your biz, all that changes:

- ♥ The copy can attract your ideal prospects.

- ♥ The copy can follow up with your ideal prospects.

- ♥ The copy can invite/have sales conversations with your ideal prospects.

- ♥ The copy can follow up until they say "yes" or "no."

Do you see how much easier marketing your biz becomes?

And even if you DO need to have a conversation to complete the sales process with a prospect, chances are the prospect will be pretty close to making a decision already, so he or she only needs a few questions answered. This means your sales calls are also much shorter.

Because direct response copy has the ability to do so much on its own, you can essentially automate your sales and marketing processes. And that's why it's at the heart of all those claims to making money on the Internet. (You know what I'm talking about — make money in your sleep, work from home in your PJs for a few hours a day and make hundreds or even thousands of dollars, etc. Of course, while there CAN be some "truth" to that claim — the REAL story is there's still a lot of hard work and long hours before you even get within shouting distance of that reality. But that's a different book for a different time.)

This is why, if you are an entrepreneur, implementing direct response copy in your biz is critical. It's how you can have a bigger reach AND enjoy more freedom. Without it, your precious time is already stretched to the limit, and your ability to get your message and gifts out into the world is severely hampered. Even if you have a strong team supporting you, you still can't replace the role direct response copy can fill in your biz.

So how can direct response possibly do all of this? Is it magic? Does it have secret powers?

No, it's not magic, even if it sometimes feels like it.

There are a couple of reasons direct response copywriting works. First, it triggers emotions in the reader, which causes them to take action (i.e. buy something). In fact, in a lot of cases it mimics our psychological buying process — the act of buying is, first and foremost, an emotional process. (We're going to get into this a lot more in the following chapters; this is just to give you a little background info.)

Basically, all emotions can be broken down into two main categories — love and fear. Love-based emotions include love, hope, gratitude, joy, connection, inspiration, peace, and respect. Fear-based emotions include fear, anger, grief, shame, guilt, blame, worry, and anxiety.

Now, the thing about fear-based emotions is they feel, well, BAD. They're uncomfortable and unpleasant, and we typically want to stop feeling them as quickly as possible.

Which is why they work so well to compel people to take action.

You see, if you stir up fear-based emotions in people, and then tell them if they take X action, those fear-based emotions will go away, then a lot of times people will take that action. It doesn't matter if you're trying to persuade people to floss more or get your kids to behave or sell a product to your ideal clients — if you trigger fear-based emotions in people, and then tell them the solution to stop feeling that emotion is to take action, in many cases they'll take the action. They just want to move away from the pain.

(There's a dirty little secret that comes with that though — the fear-based emotion doesn't actually go away with the action. It just gets buried or pushed away or numbed, which is why

16

using fear to persuade isn't a lasting or permanent solution. I'll dig into this more later in the book.)

Now, remember, buying is an emotional process. So you DO need to trigger emotions in your ideal clients. And how do you do that? By using something called "triggers" or "psychological triggers," which are basically designed to push people's hot buttons.

These triggers have been around since we were all living in caves and running away from the saber-toothed tiger, which means they're buried deep in our psyche, and in many cases are directly connected to our survival instincts.

Triggers include:

- Finding love/a relationship

- Sex appeal

- Having enough food, warmth, shelter, etc.

- Making sure our children are taken care of

- Knowing we'll be taken care of in our old age

- Being part of a community

Now, because these are connected to our survival instincts, in many cases our FEAR of losing them is stronger than our DESIRE to move toward them.

This is one of the reasons why creating fear is EASIER than creating love. (I'll get into this more later in the book, too.)

So, let's look at how you would use fear-based emotional triggers in a buying situation.

First, the fear is stirred up or agitated. The sales person tries to make the person feel as badly as possible about their current situation. After they feel pretty bad, then the sales person brings in love-based emotions as the solution.

Because, you see, what people WANT to feel are those love-based emotions. They WANT hope and transformation. People WANT to buy — they just don't want to be sold to. (Buying is fun, being sold to is not.)

So, in many traditional selling situations, sales people have mixed love and fear together. The problem is, the moment you access the fear (even if the conversation or process is, let's say, only based in about ten percent fear), the entire process will reek of fear.

And this is why so many folks are turned off by sales.

So what does this have to do with direct response copy? Well, remember, direct response copy is a way to sell one-to-many, so it makes sense that it would take a lot of its structure from good ol' selling skills. (This is why you may have heard the phrase "copywriting is salesmanship in print.") This is also why plenty of good or even excellent writers can't write a direct response page that gets results (because they lack sales skills). It's also why average or even below average writers who have strong sales skills can still get pretty decent results.

Now, that said, I want to stress (and this is REALLY important) that there is a difference between fear and pain. A lot of times fear is imaginary — but pain is not. People are in pain all the time. YOUR ideal prospects are in pain right now, and they need your gift or message to get out of it. Reminding them of their pain in order to give them the motivation to take action and get out of that pain is a gift. Scaring them because you want their money is what makes things feel "icky," and it's how direct response copy got its bad rap in the first place. (More on pain vs. pleasure later in the book.)

Now, if you're wondering how fear shows up in copy, here are a few examples of fear-based copy:

Example 1

> "You're going to have a stroke or a heart attack if you don't lose some weight."

That's what the nurse told me.

Then I eliminated this ONE food from my diet... and lost 91 pounds of fat WITHOUT "dieting" or "exercising."

You're probably eating this so-called "health food" every day, so please click the link below to read this life-saving health message now, before it's too late:

Example 2

I can't believe you still haven't activated your VIP $500-day-software we set-up for you last week... Really??

Click here to activate it now so you can finally start making some decent profits online...

Please don't put this off again. It just breaks my heart to bring something valuable to you and you just ignore it...

Are you not interested anymore?

Go here now to let me know YES or NO.

Example 3

(This last example isn't technically fear-based as it's not tapping into fear, but it is an example of the exaggeration that's so prevalent in fear-based copywriting.)

> My name is Lisa and I found the solution to dropping 17 lbs in ONE WEEK.
>
> I know this sounds like a gimmick. It isn't.
>
> In 7 short days, I was able to transform my body:
>
> → My hips went from 41" to 36"
>
> → My waist went from 34" to 30"
>
> → My body fat went from 38% down to 30%

You can feel the fear and exaggeration, right? And how does it feel? Yucky, right?

It probably makes you want to do something, anything to alleviate the fear. Like for instance — buy a product.

Poof! And that, my friends, is how direct response copy became the backbone of Internet Marketing - and ALSO how it's gotten its less-than-stellar reputation.

Because triggering fear is easier than triggering love, a lot of marketers resort to triggering fear in order to make money quickly. (While this can work in the short-term, in the long-term it can damage your brand, your reputation, your integrity and overall, your biz. More on this later.)

So rather than viewing direct response copywriting as a way to leverage yourself and your marketing so you can make a bigger impact in the world and help the people you're meant to help (which it absolutely CAN do), it's regarded as something sort of shady — full of hype and slime. It becomes something best left in the shadows of your biz. And really, something any reputable (and especially conscious or heart-centered) entrepreneur wants no part of.

Now, in my Kindle eBook, "The Dirty Little Secret About Direct Response/Internet Marketing: Why What You've Been Taught Isn't Working for You and What You Can Do to Turn it Around," I talk more about how direct response copywriting became so prevalent on the Internet and also why it triggers a negative reaction in so many entrepreneurs who consider themselves "mission driven" or "creative" or "agents of change." (You can check it out here at LoveBasedCopyBooks. com). But in a nutshell, two of the biggest reasons why entrepreneurs struggle with direct response copy are:

- 💜 It closely mimics selling skills (in other words, if you hate to sell – and a lot of conscious entrepreneurs do — you probably hate direct response copy).

- 💜 It focuses on fear, which is not in integrity with your core message that is typically around hope and love.

The selling part isn't going to change (sorry guys). Unfortunately, if you are a conscious entrepreneur and you hate to sell, this IS something you're going to have to come to terms with if you want to have a successful, profitable business that actually reaches everyone you know you're meant to reach. (HOWEVER, reading this book CAN help you with that — in fact, I have a whole section dedicated to why it's a disservice NOT to sell later in the book. The more comfortable you are with selling, the more comfortable you'll be with direct response copy.)

BUT, the second part absolutely CAN change — we CAN base direct response copy around love instead of fear. And once we do that, our resistance to selling may diminish, as well.

So what IS love-based copywriting?

Love-based copywriting still uses triggers, because you need the triggers to inspire people to take action. But rather than using triggers to make people feel fear, shame, guilt or create a false sense of urgency (which is what fear-based copywriting does), you create a buying environment that attracts and invites your ideal, perfect clients to say YES to moving forward with you.

Now, the problem with love-based copywriting is it may not be as immediately effective as fear-based. It's possible (but NOT a given) that you would make more sales using fear-based than love-based copy. But while you may make more money in the short-term, in the long-term you run the risk of eroding your business. People don't like feeling the way fear-based copywriting makes them feel, so there could be a backlash to your brand. Also, if people are buying in reaction to painful emotions, you could end up attracting the wrong clients, which is just about the last thing you want to do, because clients who are wrong for you will probably take more of your time and energy to make happy, and after all of that, they STILL won't be happy and may refund and/or tell people they had a bad experience with you (which can also impact future sales).

So to sum it up — when you use fear-based copywriting, you MAY make more sales, but you also may end up with a higher percentage of refunds and unhappy clients, not to mention experiencing a slow erosion of your brand.

With love-based copywriting, you MAY make less overall sales, but you're far more likely to attract the perfect people into your programs, who will be a joy to work with, who will do everything you say, experience huge transformation, and become your raving fans.

And that's not all! Love-based copywriting also has the power to grow your brand in a more powerful way.

(Doesn't that feel just so yummy perfect?)

So if you're ready to become part of the transformation of direct response copywriting ... if you're ready to learn how to use love and respect to increase your reach and visibility while growing your business, keep reading! Because the exciting news is you absolutely CAN. And this book is going to show you how.

Love-Based Copywriting Method:

Chapter 2
IT ALL STARTS WITH WORDS

When you're sitting down to write love-based copy, one of the most crucial elements is making sure you mindset or "come from" is aligned with love and abundance. I devote an entire chapter to this later in the book, but for right now I want to cover Internet Marketing vocabulary, because understanding the terminology is an important first step.

As traditional sales and marketing relies on tapping into fear-based emotions, there are a lot of "dehumanizing" words associated with it — "leads," "squeeze pages," "list," etc. And, when you think about it, it makes sense. If you're going to purposely trigger fear-based emotions in your customers in order to compel them to buy, you really don't want to consider what you're doing to actual human beings.

Now, I want to stress, I don't think this was done intentionally nor do I think anyone is "bad" for doing it. I go into more detail around the "why folks market this way" later in the book.

But, as we move into the love-based philosophy, we want to be mindful about our own mindset and actions, and changing our own language around common Internet Marketing terms is a great first step to help you move into that space of love and abundance.

So without further ado, let's jump in.

Website — So the "official" definition is a collection of web pages that lives on the Internet and provides a broad overview of your business.

However, here in love-based copywriting land, we shift that definition a bit. Here, a website is an "online showroom."

If you had a "bricks and mortar" business, you would have a showroom where you could invite your ideal prospects to sit down, have a cup of tea and talk about how your biz could help them solve what's keeping them up at night. Right?

Well, your "online showroom" serves the exact same purpose. Your website is essentially an invitation to your ideal prospects to stop in for a cup of tea and a chat to see if what you sell is the perfect fit for what they are looking for.

(And yes, it really IS a 2-way conversation — as your ideal prospects read, they're having a conversation in their head with your copy, and if they decide they're done, the conversation is over.)

Branding/Taglines/Logos — I define branding as the overall feeling people have around your business, which is usually based on their experience with it. It includes things like (but is not limited to) logos and taglines. Logos are graphical representations of your business while taglines are brief word descriptions.

I know lots of entrepreneurs get hung up on taglines and logos, and while having both is never a bad idea since they can certainly help your business (I personally have a logo I love — my exclamation point) they aren't necessary to actually making money. If you're just starting out, I wouldn't worry much about a logo or tagline. Instead, I'd focus more on other direct response pieces (such as a really good opt-in page and freebie — see below) to start building my community and making money.

Sales Letters (also known as long-copy sales letters or long-form sales letters) — These are the super-long pages on the Internet where you scroll down for what seems like forever looking for a price.

Now, in the land of love-based copywriting, I want you to think about these online sales letters as "departments" in your online showroom, because these pages are how you sell specific products, programs, events, etc.

Emails — Emails (or electronic mail) can be used for all sorts of things — staying in touch with old friends, communicating with clients, or marketing to your ideal prospects. In love-based copywriting, I like to think of emails as sales representatives who direct your ideal prospects to the perfect department (i.e. sales letter) for them.

Opt-in Page/Landing Page/Squeeze Page — All of these titles refer to the exact same thing: a page that asks for a name and email in exchange for something free. If you're offering a free call or webinar, or a special report pdf, or a recording of a training (or any other type of free offer), you would likely use an opt-in page to collect information.

Here in love-based copywriting land, I prefer the term "opt-in page" (which is the term we'll use throughout this book) because it best reflects the actual process: your ideal prospects choose to give you their contact info and start a relationship with you. ("Squeeze page" in particular is a very manipulative term, as it refers to the page "squeezing" the contact information out of people.) I also like to think of opt-in pages as the "line outside your online showroom."

Ideal Clients/Ideal Prospects — This one is so important I've devoted the next chapter entirely to how to find your ideal clients, but I wanted to at least get the conversation started with a quick definition. Here in the land of love-based copywriting, we prefer the terms "ideal clients" for customers and "ideal prospects" for leads.

I don't like "leads" because it depersonalizes your prospects — and once you've depersonalized your prospects, it's not a leap to then depersonalize your customers. You might even start thinking of them as "walking wallets." (And once you start thinking about your customers as "walking wallets," it's a lot easier to use fear-based direct response tactics since you're only thinking about trying to squeeze as much money out of them as you can — you don't really care about how they feel.)

The term "customers" doesn't really bother me, but I think it's more powerful to get into the habit of calling your customers "ideal clients" or "ideal customers," because it's actually a lot easier to write copy and create marketing campaigns that attract your ideal clients versus attracting just anyone who is willing to pay you money regardless of whether or not he/she is a good fit for you and your business. (Yes! It really is! Keep reading to find out why and how.)

Community/List – "List" is an old term, which basically refers to a list of folks you can contact — in many cases it's a list of email addresses. Since so much of online marketing depends on sending emails, the more email addresses you have (i.e. the bigger list), the more desirable of a joint venture or affiliate partner you are. (Joint venture and affiliates are folks who promote your products and services and you pay them a commission for every sale that comes out of their promotion. The difference between joint venture and affiliates typically is the level of promotion and commitment — joint venture partners typically act more like actual partners, and the two of you will work harder to promote each other to your respective communities, whereas affiliates are typically less committed to you and the promotion.)

Now I don't like "list," because it also depersonalizes your ideal prospects. All of a sudden they are reduced to an email address — not living, breathing people. That's why I like "community."

Plus, "community" is all-encompassing. Your promotional efforts can be much bigger than simply a list of emails you have permission to mail to. Your community includes your Twitter and Facebook friends, blog readers, podcast listeners, video watchers, etc. Really, anyone who is following you (no matter what medium they choose) is part of your community.

Conversions — The holy grail of direct response — direct response copy lives and dies by conversion rate. Conversion rate refers to the percentage of folks who read your copy and take the desired action (ie. how many visitors to your website give you their email address, how many people who read your sales letter buy your product, etc.). Conversion rates vary depending upon what you're asking people to do (i.e. click on a link in an email, give you their email address or get out their credit card to buy something). For instance, a good conversion rate for a sales letter is 1% — that means 1 out of every 100 people who visit your sales letter buy.

If you're asking folks to do something that's free (i.e. give you their email address in exchange for something like a special report or webinar) you should have a higher conversion rate than 1%, but there's a huge variation because there are so many other factors. In some cases, you might see 20%-30% conversions on opt-ins (i.e. using a paid Facebook ad campaign that sends new "colder" visitors to your website, who may never have heard of you before so they may be less likely to opt-in for your freebie) to 60% or higher (i.e. having an affiliate/JV partner send an email to their list or you send an email to your list to an opt-in page, because the people who click on those links are much warmer as they would have some sort of relationship with you or your affiliate/JV partner, so they are more likely to opt-in).

Headlines — The big words at the top of the page. On "Planet Direct Response Copywriting," the point of the headline is to get folks to start reading the copy. That's it. (And that's actually a pretty big job as typically 80% of the people who end up reading copy say they based their decision to start reading on the headline.)

Because headlines are so critical to the success of a direct response piece (as you can imagine, it's tough to get someone to do something if they don't read anything) headlines are one of the first things people test when they're trying to improve conversions.

In addition to headlines, there are also pre-heads (you can find pre-heads above the headlines, typically they're in a smaller font and they may also be highlighted) and subheads (these are found below the headline and also can be used to break up longer pieces of copy).

Call to Action (CTA) — Just as you always find headlines at the top of a piece of copy, a call to action is found at the bottom. A call to action is exactly that — you're making a call for people to take your desired action. It could be to buy something, it could be to send an email, it could be to fill out a form, it could be to click on a link or give you an email address, etc. There are lots and lots of different types of CTAs, but the most important thing to remember is you MUST include one if you're writing direct response copy.

Features/Benefits — So it's important to begin a piece of copy with a headline and end it with a CTA, but what about the muddy middle? Ah, that's where features and benefits come in.

You use features and benefits to describe your product/service/program/etc. Features are the service delivery – what you're actually selling. Is it a book? A CD set? An event? A coaching program?

Now, while people DO need to know what they're buying, they aren't really buying a bunch of CDs or a chance to yak with you on the phone. What they're really buying is the outcome, the transformation, the solution to their problem. So you need to describe what you're selling to your ideal clients in a way that clearly explains "what's in it for them." This is what is known as benefits.

90% of the description of your product should be about the benefits, and 10% should be about the features. What typically happens when entrepreneurs are first starting out is that 90%

of the description is around the features and 10% is around the benefits. Even seasoned entrepreneurs (who really ought to know better) struggle with this, so you're not alone if this doesn't come as easily to you as you'd like.

Why? Well I think it's a couple of things. First, as the creator of the product/program/service, you are far more focused on the features than the benefits, so that's what pops up first in your head. (Especially if this is a product that's taken awhile to actually birth — the more time you spent on it, the more you want people to know how involved and in-depth it is.) Second, it's definitely a lot easier to write features than benefits – the features merely describe what people actually get (remember – a book / CD / program). Benefits require you to dig deeper – to get under the surface and at the heart of WHY someone should spend their hard-earned money to buy your offering. That takes more work than simply describing what the program is. Note — if you are looking for more "nuts and bolts" copywriting teaching, make sure you check out Volume 2 of my Love-Based Business series: "The Love-Based Copywriting System." That's where I go into much more detail about how to actually write headlines, calls to action, features/ benefits and the other essential direct response copy elements.

So that covers basic copywriting terms. Let's move on to the heart of what puts the "love" in love-based copywriting, starting with ideal clients.

Chapter 3
IDEAL CLIENTS

Knowing who your ideal clients are is not only critical to writing love-based copy, but also to building a successful, profitable, love-based business. This is why I've devoted an entire chapter to finding and understanding your ideal client.

Let's start by talking about what makes ideal clients different from target markets or niche markets. Target markets (the customers your business serves) typically are more demographically based — for instance, your target market may be stay-at-home moms between the ages of 30 and 50.

Niche markets take target markets one step further by refining and specializing who you're selling to. A niche market may be stay-at-home moms, between the ages of 30 and 50, who are looking for a home-based business opportunity.

The reason a lot of marketers recommend "niche-ing" down your target market is because the more focused you are when it comes to who you're selling to, the easier it is to sell to them. If everyone you're selling to has some common ground you can speak to, the easier it is to market and sell to them, because you can emphasize that common ground. In addition, even though it sounds counter-intuitive, when you try to sell to everyone, you actually end up selling to nobody. Why? Well a couple of reasons.

First, if you're trying to sell to everyone, you're probably getting pretty generic. And the more generic you get, the less people are going to recognize their SPECIFIC problem in your generic description. Remember, your ideal clients live in a world of specifics — their problem is very real and very specific to them. In fact, they may even go as far as to say "but MY situation/problem is different/unique etc." They only see what makes them unique, not what they have in common with others who have their same problem.

That's why if you are equally specific, they'll recognize themselves in your copy and think "Wow, I can see myself here," or "She's really talking to me." If you stay in the land of generalities, you run the very real risk of them walking right by your marketing materials, because they don't recognize themselves or their problem in them.

In addition, when people are ready to solve a problem, they tend to (but not always) want to hire a specialist. Because once they've decided they're ready to get rid of the problem, they don't want to waste their time and money on something that may not work for them (and when things are generic, they don't always work for specific cases, especially if those specific cases are more complicated or difficult than generic cases.). So they're going to, as much as possible, try and work with the specialist, so they can finally solve those problems once and for all.

Now, while I agree with the concept of niche markets, I don't like niche markets alone because I don't think they go deep enough. That's where the concept of ideal client comes in.

You see, the problem with niche markets and target markets is they're based too much on external factors — i.e. demographic info. Ideal clients, on the other hand, are defined by internal factors — values, motivations, and core beliefs.

The more you can tune into what's going on in your clients' head, the easier it will be to attract them, because they'll feel like you really "get" them. Also, knowing who your ideal clients are and specifically writing to them in your copy is one of the key principles of writing love-based copy.

So what does focusing on internal factors mean, exactly? Well, remember my niche market example — stay-at-home moms looking for a home-based business opportunity? There are actually two ideal client groups in that one niche market.

The first ideal client group consists of mothers who are looking for a biz opportunity because they want something for themselves. They feel like their entire lives are wrapped around taking care of other people and that they're losing their identity as a person. Their financial needs are met, so they don't necessarily need the income (although they may want the income) but mostly what they're looking for is something just for them.

Now, just because they're looking for something for themselves doesn't mean they want to ignore their family. Au Contraire — being there for their family is very important, so this biz opportunity must be flexible. They need to be able to do it when they can fit it into their busy lives. They still want to cook dinner and cheer at soccer games and pick up the dry cleaning. So this business opportunity needs to fit into the open time pockets they have throughout their days.

Okay so that's ideal client group 1. Ideal client group 2 consists of moms who have found themselves in a situation where they need to be the bread winner. They are looking for a biz opportunity that will pay the mortgage and put food on the table, and they want that to happen as fast as possible. While having a flexible work schedule is nice, they don't necessarily mind putting in long hours if they'll be able to support their family. So for them, what's most important is how much money they can make with this biz opportunity.

So think about these two ideal client groups. Do you see how different they are? And do you see how different the messages to each of them would need to be? (Ideal client 1 would be all about flexibility and having something for herself while ideal client 2 would be all about how much and how fast she can make money.) Yet on the surface they're in the same niche market. That's why taking that next step and moving from niche markets to ideal client is so crucial.

Now, you may be thinking — why do I have to make a choice? Why can't I put BOTH messages into my copy?

Well, the problem is if you try to talk to both groups, you'll likely talk to neither. Because ideal client 1 is not motivated by money, any messages about money wouldn't land for her. She might feel like the biz opportunity wouldn't be all that flexible after all and she would have to compromise her family duties. And ideal client 2 may read about the flexibility and be concerned she won't make the money she needs to make after all, and look elsewhere.

Think about yourself as a consumer. When you're looking for a product or service to solve a problem you have, you want it to be as specific to your problem as possible, right? Likely you aren't looking for a general solution because a general solution may not solve your SPECIFIC problem — and you don't want to spend the time or money screwing around with something that won't actually take care of your problem.

That's what your ideal clients will feel if they read too many messages in your copy — even if your solution really CAN solve the problems of multiple people, they may just not believe it. (Or, what they likely will believe is your solution can solve OTHER people's problems, just not THEIR SPECIFIC problems.)

Now, one reason entrepreneurs want to have multiple messages in their copy is because they're worried their ideal client group is too small. What if they don't have enough clients? What if they end up turning good-paying clients away?

Those fears are completely normal and natural, so let's talk about why attracting ideal clients will actually make your business more profitable (not to mention enjoyable) than selling to anyone and everyone.

1. You actually will attract more clients being more specific with your messaging than being generic. I touched on this in the messaging part but to reiterate — the more specific your messaging, the more likely your ideal clients will recognize you are talking specifically to them, and they'll be less likely to walk past your copy to find their solution with someone else (who, chances are, is being more specific). Remember, being specific implies you're more of an expert (think specialist versus generalist) and for the most part, people would prefer to work with a specialist than a generalist.

2. Serving just your ideal clients will be more profitable than trying to serve everyone. One of the main benefits around serving only your ideal clients is you're working with folks who love you, love what you do, who YOU love, and they typically end up becoming your raving fans and telling all their friends about you. When you work with people who are not your ideal clients, that's when you end up with people you dread talking to, who are difficult (if not impossible) to please, who you end up jumping through

tons of hoops to make happy…and they STILL aren't happy, and after ALL of that, they may even end up asking for a refund.

It's that whole 80-20 rule — 20% of your clients cause 80% of your work. And typically the 20% who are causing 80% of your work are not your ideal clients.

Now, of course if you're experiencing a slow time in your biz and a non-ideal client shows up on your doorstep, you may decide you're okay with it — but overall your business will be more profitable if you don't have the extra work, time and energy drag that comes from working with people who just aren't a good fit. (And you'll actually be doing everyone a favor by releasing them and allowing them to find the person they're meant to work with. Wouldn't you want your counterpart to release people who aren't their ideal clients but are YOUR ideal clients so they could come find you? Everyone would be happier and better served.)

3. In most cases, once you make a point of attracting your ideal clients into your business, you'll likely find there are more than enough of them to fill your business. You'd have to serve a super tiny ideal client group for that not to be the case (and I haven't seen anyone serve a group quite that small).

Now, if for some reason you do find you're in the minority and your ideal client group is too small, here's what I would suggest: first off, don't beat yourself up. The fact that you now KNOW is a good thing — you wouldn't have known if you hadn't tried it. So the next thing is to either switch to a different ideal client group (chances are you have a few different types of folks you enjoy working with) or simply add to or expand the current ideal client group.

Testing and tweaking is a part of marketing, and no matter how big you get, you're still going to run into a product not selling well or a marketing campaign not doing as well as you thought — this is just what happens when you're an entrepreneur.

So now that you know why building your marketing around your ideal clients is so important, are you ready to figure out who your ideal client is?

Great!

EXERCISE

To start, I want you to close your eyes and think about your favorite client. It doesn't have to be someone who even paid you; it could someone you helped for free.

Once you have him/her in your head, get out a pen and paper and start describing him. Be as specific as possible. What is it about him that made him your favorite client to work with?

What did you really appreciate about him? What did he appreciate about you?

Don't rush this process — take all the time you need to really get a good sense of who your ideal client really is.

Once you have a strong sense of who your ideal clients are, not only will you be in a position to write really powerful copy to attract them (more on that in later chapters) but you'll also have a much better idea of where to find them. Instead of wasting time and money on places where your ideal clients aren't hanging out (and worse, you don't even know they aren't there because you haven't done this work), you can instead focus on where your ideal clients actually are.

And it doesn't stop there — you'll also have a better idea of which products or services to sell them, how you need to set up your business to better serve them, etc. That's why knowing who your ideal clients are is so important to all aspects of your business.

So what happens if, as you complete this exercise, you realize you have multiple ideal clients? As my earlier example around the stay-at-home moms showed, you really need different copy pieces to speak to each specific ideal client group. So even though technically you can have as many as you want, since it is a lot of work to set up different pages for each ideal client group, I would suggest you pick one and go (or "pick a horse and ride it" as the saying goes). You can always add a second one later if you're so inclined.

Now, we're going to keep returning to ideal clients throughout the rest of the book, so if you haven't done the exercise, I would encourage you to take 10 minutes right now and do so before moving to the next chapter. You'll get far more out of the rest of the book if you can start thinking about the principles I talk about with your specific ideal clients in mind.

Chapter 4
PAIN VERSUS PLEASURE

Now that you know who your ideal clients are, the next step is to start connecting with them. And the first step in that process is to identify their pain.

If you're like so many of the conscious, heart-centered entrepreneurs out there, the thought of talking about your ideal clients' pain makes you want to run for the hills. You're trying to ALLEVIATE pain — the last thing you want is for your copy and marketing to be about the very thing you want to heal.

Okay, so first off, I get it. Yes, talking about other people's pain (much less mucking around in it so you make people feel worse) is uncomfortable at best and truly awful at worse.

But, let's talk about it - because there are a few things you may not have considered:

1. There IS a difference between pain and suffering. Pain is real — there is a problem in people's lives and they experience pain around it. In fact, I would even take it a step further to say that pain is NECESSARY. There are people who are born who can't feel physical pain and they tend to not live long. Their body can't tell them when something is wrong so they can fix it.

We need pain to keep us healthy physically, and we need pain to help us grow emotionally and spiritually.

But suffering is another story. Suffering typically happens in our heads — we magnify the pain with fear, shame, guilt or something else, and we suffer.

Pain is a part of life. Suffering doesn't have to be.

It's one thing to remind people of their pain so they can decide if they're either ready to find a solution for the pain or if they're not ready to move forward quite yet. If they're done with the pain, they may be ready for your product or service. If not, they're probably not ideal clients yet.

As part of the love-based copywriting approach, reminding folks of their pain is an important part of the process (which I get into more below). Twisting the knife so you cause suffering is not (and a lot of traditional direct response copywriting has roots in twisting the knife as much as possible, which is one of the reasons why it feels so yucky). It's a fine line, but a crucial one, and I'll talk more about how to walk that fine line.

2. Pain adds urgency. You would never call your dentist in the middle of the night and say "Oh my God, I missed my teeth cleaning, can you get me in now?" But if you broke a tooth? Or a jaw? Yeah, you'd likely be willing to wake your dentist (or doctor) up. This is why the following saying exists: "We're more likely to move away from pain than

we are toward pleasure." Remember, one of the main purposes of pain is to act as your alarm system to let you know when something is wrong so you can fix it. That's why when we feel pain, one of our first responses is to try and figure out what's causing it. Moving toward pleasure doesn't have that same power — sure, we'd love to experience more pleasure, but that urgency to make sure there isn't something seriously wrong isn't there. (This is why trying to sell without respectfully discussing your ideal client's pain is difficult.)

If you don't remind your ideal clients about their pain, they may say things like "Oh what you do sounds great; I'll definitely have to work with you one day." And of course, they never do.

But that doesn't mean the pain goes away. On the contrary, you may actually end up causing suffering, because your ideal clients don't know that working with you will actually alleviate their pain.

Look, people stand in their own way all the time. And unless you actually remind them they truly are IN pain while they're reading about your offering, they will be far more likely to brush it under the rug: "Oh, it's fine — I can deal with it for another few months until the kids are in school/out of school/ after the holidays/etc." Only by reminding them will you give them the gift of being able to choose — do they really want to stay there? Or are they ready to move forward?

3. People are busy. If you aren't clear about reiterating WHAT their pain is (so they know you "get" their pain) and WHY your product or service will solve that pain, they'll probably walk right by you, still searching for the person who can solve their pain.

4. Remember, the copy on your websites and sales letters (and really anywhere else) is part of a 2-way conversation taking place in your ideal client's head. So, you need to start the conversation where your ideal clients are — and where they typically are is in their pain. They know what their problem is and they're looking for a solution. Now, most of the time they have no idea what the solution is, so if you skip the pain and start with your offerings, again they won't have any idea that what you sell will actually take care of their problem, so they won't "get" that you're talking to them. Their pain, on the other hand, they ARE familiar with. So you want to start with their pain so you are actually starting at the beginning of the conversation (if you start anywhere else, your ideal client may feel like she walked into the middle of a conversation). Plus, this is how she'll also know she's in exactly the right place.

5. Because I know talking about pain can trigger negative feelings for some entrepreneurs, I would love for you to shift your perspective a bit. Ask yourself this: "What's keeping my ideal clients up at night?" Once you identify that, you can clearly see how your solution will help them sleep better. And if you convey that, you're definitely

headed in the right direction – the direction of love-based copywriting.

Honestly, it's really a disservice NOT to mention your ideal client's pain. Think of it as tough love — parents know they sometimes have to touch on their children's pain points in order to help them learn and grown. You're doing the same. Life isn't about feeling good all the time and if we deny the pain, we're adding to the problem, not solving it.

I'm also a big believer that the sales process should mirror the transformation your ideal clients will get working with you. And if you are a transformative teacher or coach, you already know there's going to be some pain when folks transform. If you don't give them the gift of going through their pain in your marketing or selling process, they may decide in the middle of working with you they're not ready to move forward — and that's when people disappear, drop out or even ask for refunds (and none of us want those things to happen).

At the end of the day, what you need to keep in mind is this — it's a disservice to not mention your ideal client's pain and it's also a disservice if you aren't respectful of their pain when you mention it.

Okay, so now that you're (hopefully) on board with acknowledging the pain, let's talk more about logistics.

First off, while I want you to talk about what's keeping your ideal clients up at night, I don't want you to wallow in it. My standard rule of thumb is around 30% (or even less) of any piece of copy should touch on pain — the other 70% should focus on pleasure/results/transformation/hope.

THAT'S love-based copywriting.

What people want to buy is transformation. Buying is fun (being sold to is not) and they want to buy the transformation. If you keep flogging the pain, that's not fun and they'll eventually stop reading and click away.

Typically it works well to start with the pain — remember, you want to start the conversation where they're at. And when you write about it, just describe it as objectively as possible. What are they dealing with every day? What's going on in their heads?

Where it turns into suffering is when you go overboard and start describing worst case scenarios or the "blood in the streets." One example where you often see this is in copy promoting financial advice — "The whole world is going to crash and burn and only I know what to do so you don't lose everything and end up in the streets with the rest of the rabble fighting over crusts of bread!" This is a great example of what I would consider the wrong way to use pain, which is more like "future spinning" — not just describing how pain is showing up in their lives right now, but taking it a few steps further to describe the worst, most dreadful outcome.

The way I like to do it is to use 3-5 bullets describing a few scenarios that are keeping my ideal prospects up at night, and then I start moving to the solution/transformation. I'll probably go back to some pain points later in the copy — just as a reminder of what they're going to be stuck in if they choose not to do something to solve their problem. (In other words, it also creates a sense of urgency — so people feel compelled to move forward NOW rather than waiting for the "perfect" time.)

Here's an example of what I'm talking about, from my Why Isn't My Website Making Me Any Money? sales letter:

> In fact, maybe some of the following sounds familiar to you, too:
>
> ♥ You've spent thousands of dollars or hundreds of hours (or both) putting up a website only to find it doesn't do much of anything for you. You feel stuck and frustrated because not only are you not reaching the people you're meant to help, but also, the money is gone and you're not getting a return on your investment.

💜 You have a genuine passion for helping people, and you know your products and programs will provide solutions that will improve lives. But something about your website just isn't clicking, because none of your prospects are buying! Making a big impact is trickier than you'd expected, and you're feeling discouraged.

💜 You know you should be doing something to make your website and marketing efforts pay off, but you aren't sure what that is. You've done tons of reading, and all the gurus and experts give different, conflicting advice. You've become "paralyzed" in overwhelm, so you don't do anything.

💜 You've tried a bunch of different marketing tactics already —emails, newsletter, giveaways, social networking… everything you thought you were "supposed to" do—but nothing seems to be working to increase your profits.

💜 To make matters worse, no one can really tell you WHY your website isn't effective! You feel like you're spinning your wheels, instead of supporting others the way you so badly want to.

See how those bullets talk about the pain without causing suffering?

Lastly, let's talk about HOW to identify your ideal client's pain.

EXERCISE

First, if you haven't figured out who your ideal client is, now is an excellent time to complete the ideal client exercise. If you have done it, take a moment to review your notes and "see" your ideal client clearly in your head.

Now, get a pen and paper and start answering the "What is keeping my ideal clients up at night?" question. Start writing everything they might be thinking. Don't hold back, don't try and censor and, above all, don't put it into "marketing speak." What are the actual words they would be saying? That's what you want to get to the heart of — not a summary of what their pain is but how they would describe their pain themselves, if they were talking to a friend.

THOSE are the words you want to use in your marketing copy.

You can also ask your current ideal clients what was keeping them up at night and why they decided to hire you. Write down EXACTLY what they say — their words and their phrasing. You want to mirror how they're thinking as closely as possible so they immediately recognize they're in the right place when they read your marketing copy.

Now, for some of you, this may be easier because the pain you solve is a more "urgent" pain — for instance, you help people make more money. But even if you offer something that is less urgent — like you sell toys for instance — there is still something that keeps your ideal clients up at night.

I worked with a client once who sold kits that allowed grandparents to write a book with their grandchildren. On the surface, it doesn't seem like there would be much that would keep the grandparents up at night. But if you dig a little deeper, there is definitely something — these kits provide a wonderful way to create lasting memories with their grandchildren. Grandparents can spend precious time with their grandchildren. And it allows them to share their own stories about growing up so they aren't lost.

Grandparents who long to create a deep, lasting connecting with their grandchildren and have a way to share their experiences and knowledge with their grandchildren are her ideal clients. And the pain of course is feeling like they're missing that connection and running out of time to share their stories.

You see how that works?

So even if it isn't immediately obvious, I would love to challenge you to sit with this exercise and really think about it. Once you scratch beneath the surface, you may be amazed by what comes out.

Chapter 5
WHAT IS YOUR "COME FROM" WHEN YOU MARKET?

One of the biggest keys to love-based copywriting is to take a hard look at both your mindset and "come from." Nail this and the rest of love-based copywriting starts falling right into place.

So what exactly do I mean by this?

Let's start with your "come from."

"Come from" refers to how you are approaching the copy you're writing (or have written). Are you coming from a place that's in line with the principles I've talked about in this book? From a place of abundance, love and wanting to attract your perfect, ideal client and trusting that this will work out to everyone's highest good? Or are you coming from a place where you want to make money "above all else"?

Now, before we go any further, I want to say a few words about making money — starting with I WANT you to make money. Look, the whole definition of being in business is to make money (otherwise you've either started a nonprofit association or you have a hobby), so you most definitely should be profitable and making money. Period.

In addition, if you're someone who wants to do more "good" in the world (i.e. give money away to worthy causes or perhaps even start your own nonprofit association) the more money you make, the more good you can do. So, if you look at it that way, not having a successful business that takes care of your financial needs and that provides you with the means to help others, if you so choose, is a disservice.

And my personal take is it makes good business sense to embrace the love-based copywriting principles in order to increase your profits. As I talked about earlier, love-based copywriting means you're attracting your perfect, ideal clients, who will rave about you, be easy for you to work with and won't be asking for refunds. And all that means your business will be far more profitable and less exhausting than a business filled with less-than-ideal clients. You also are more likely to build a solid, respectful brand (which can go a long way to help convince new ideal clients to give your products and services a try). And let's not forget, if you're someone who has a bigger mission — i.e. you want to transform the world or at the very least leave it in a better state than you found it, you probably resonate with building a biz based on love versus fear. I'm of the belief that you can't have a love-based business unless every part of your business is love-based (if even 10% of your marketing is based in fear, the whole thing is tainted with fear). So if you're not bringing your ideal clients into your business with love, you can't possibly have a love-based business.

BUT that means you must be willing to be fine with whatever happens during a promotion — even if that means you have less ideal clients who raise their hands to work with you than you wanted, not to mention being willing to let the less-than-ideal clients go even if they're willing to hand over their cash.

And that's what I mean by "making money above all else" — it's not a judgment around making money. It's a fact — you're willing to compromise everything including your time, energy, and maybe even some "long-term" profit in order to make more money now.

Now, I totally get this can feel really scary. Especially if your business isn't doing so hot right now.

The problem is, you can't "come from" a place of wanting to only attract, inspire and invite your ideal prospects to become your ideal clients if your mindset is one of fear, anxiety and worry about paying your bills. If you're worried about making money, no matter how good your intentions may be, it will be extremely difficult to be okay with letting less-than-ideal clients go.

And if you can't let them go, you'll be more likely to fall into using guilt, shame, fear, arm-twisting, or any other fear-based tactic that will work, just so you can "close the sale."

(It's a vicious cycle, isn't it?)

So what are your options?

To start, if your business is making money right now, it will be much easier for you to embrace the love-based copywriting mindset, so let's start with that.

Before you sit down to create a marketing campaign, close your eyes, take a few deep breaths, and really feel into the space of attracting, inspiring and inviting your ideal clients to join you. Feel them out there. Feel what they're looking for from you.

Once you can really feel into that, open your eyes and start writing TO them. BUT I want you to write to only ONE ideal client.

Not a group of them. Only one specific person. (In fact, I want you to go as far as seeing a name and person in your mind.)

And I want you to write to this one, single, specific ideal client as you would to a friend.

You know your friend is in pain. And you know you have the solution to get her out of pain. So wouldn't you be passionate about describing how your solution will help her because you just KNOW how much her life will transform?

Now clearly, you can't use this letter to your friend verbatim in your copy. What I want you to do is take that energy - that love-based wording - and put it in direct response copywriting format. Consider the letter to your friend a first draft; then go back and revise it. (If you'd like a step-by-step system to help you turn that passion into a copywriting format that attracts, inspires and invites, you may want to consider getting my "Love-Based Copywriting System" book — learn more at LoveBasedCopyBooks.com.)

Now, if the first part of this exercise sounds sort of woo-woo to you and you don't think you're feeling anything, that's okay too. A big part of this exercise is to get YOU into the space of welcoming your perfect, ideal clients. Because when you do that, you'll naturally start to reject phrases and word choices that don't feel in alignment with attracting, inviting and inspiring your ideal prospects to become ideal clients.

You'll be okay with letting less-than-ideal clients go, and by letting them go, you're opening the space for the perfect ones to walk on through. (Plus, you'll probably also start to naturally choose language that more specifically attracts your ideal clients.)

So now let's look at what you can do if you really need to attract money right now.

First off, there's nothing wrong with that. We've all been there. There is nothing to be ashamed of if you need your business to generate more cash.

The first thing you need to do is put together a focused plan. What is your plan to make the money? Are you planning on launching a new product or program? Are you going to be attending an event to attract new clients?

Now, I want you to make a conscious decision. Do you want to embrace love-based copywriting principles? Or are you willing to do "whatever it takes" to make the money?

There is no right or wrong choice here — but I want you to make a conscious choice. What I don't want you to do is to fall into fear-based copywriting because you didn't make a conscious choice about what you wanted to do.

I also want you to think about this — what happens if your plan doesn't work? What is your Plan B? (Big note here — as I already discussed, using fear-based copy MAY increase your initial sales...but it also may NOT. There are no guarantees here. So keep this in mind as you think through possibilities.)

Really take some time to consider this thoroughly so you can fully step into your choice.

Why am I being such a stickler about this? Because when you make choices subconsciously or you THINK you've made a choice to do something one way but you've subconsciously chosen a different path, things really get messed up. Disasters happen, the Universe brings out the 2x4, and suddenly you've made things a lot more difficult for yourself.

One clear sign you've fallen into fear-based tactics without consciously choosing to is if you find yourself making excuses — "Well, I can handle it," "It won't be so bad," "I know my program is really good and I'm sure it will help them even though it doesn't seem like they're my ideal client." If you hear yourself saying things like this, then you're probably making a subconscious choice – or you're about to.

What I would like to suggest you do instead is to not make an excuse but instead make a choice. You're choosing to do X — such as accept a less-than-ideal client and you're doing so because of X reason and you know it may be difficult but you're willing to accept the consequences because you feel like the consequences are less painful than not accepting this less-than-ideal client in the first place.

And when you make a decision from that energy, you are far less likely to end up with a disaster on your hands.

Now what if your conscious choice is to move beyond the fear and embrace love-based copywriting? What do you do to change your mindset from fear to love, and really feel that abundance and wealth will follow, even if you can't see it right now?

What helps here is any exercise that can help you expand, open up and feel abundant. So, for instance, exercises that tap into the law of attraction can work really well. I've also included a list below to get you started:

💜 Gratitude (making lists of what you feel grateful for and really feeling into being grateful)

💜 Meditation

💜 Journaling

💜 Affirmations — the actual definition of an affirmation, according to Webster's Dictionary, is "A statement asserting the existence or the truth of something." Basically, we say affirmations to ourselves every day, both positive and negative ("X always happens to me"). The practice of using affirmations to tap into the law of attraction is to purposefully craft a statement in present tense, that's positive, personal and specific. And once you craft it, say it to yourself over and over (say it out loud, in your head, write it down, etc.)

Below are some sample affirmations to get you started (and feel free to write your own; remember, being personal with your affirmations is important):

💜 I attract wealth and abundance easily and effortlessly.

💜 Wealth and abundance come easily to me.

- 💜 I attract my most perfect ideal clients easily and effortlessly.

- 💜 My business is filled with the most perfect ideal clients.

- 💜 Rituals to cleanse old energy that is no longer serving you and welcome in new energy.

- 💜 Grounding yourself — stand outside in your bare feet touching earth and relax. (Stand on the ground for at least 10 minutes. You may want to listen to music you enjoy as you do this.)

Also, depending on how stuck you feel, you may want to work with a coach or a program to bust through those mindset blocks. You can find resources on my blog — MichelePW.com/blog, including episodes of my PW Unplugged Radio where I interview top mindset coaches and experts.

Chapter 6
THE PHILOSOPHY BEHIND SELLING IN A LOVE-BASED WAY

Remember, buying is an emotional experience.

People love to buy, hate to be sold to, and absolutely abhor feeling manipulated.

And that, my friends, in a nutshell is why direct response copywriting has gotten such a bad rap.

Again, for years entrepreneurs used fear-based tactics to get people to buy, triggering feelings of fear, shame, guilt, anger and more. Now they did NOT do that because they necessarily enjoyed it, but because that was what was commonly taught. And the reason why it was taught was because it worked. And since a lot of copywriting teachers subscribed to the principle, "Why mess with something that works?," they kept teaching it.

In addition, a lot of marketers who are truly okay using fear typically fall into the "ends justify the means" camp. To them, all is fair in love and war, just as long as you join their program or buy their product.

And while there is no question there are folks out there selling crap, who are only in it to make as much money as fast as possible, I believe the vast majority of fear-based marketers truly feel their product or program will make a difference.

They're selling a quality product and they want as many people to benefit from it as possible — yes, because they'll make more money, but also because they truly want to help as many people as possible.

But, even though their hearts may be in the right place, I don't believe it works like that. You see, I don't believe the ends justify the means — I believe how you bring your ideal clients into your business sets the tone for your future relationship. If you bring them in with fear, fear will hover over your relationship. How will they fully trust you when they hit a rough patch? Would they be able to come to you openly and willingly for help? Will they give you the benefit of the doubt if your company doesn't measure up or makes a mistake? Or will they never quite trust you — viewing everything you do with skepticism — believing you're only trying to sell them *more*, as opposed to actually trying to help them solve their problem?

Remember, when you trigger fear in your prospects so they buy to get themselves out of fear, they really aren't dealing with the emotion. Instead they're running from it or burying it or numbing it, and now your company is all mixed up with that.

This is why, for many fear-based companies, they subscribe to the theory that if you don't have a 10% return rate, you're not selling enough. If you sell with fear, you're going to have a higher return rate, because the whole point of selling with fear is to sell as much as possible to as many as possible, regardless if you're attracting your ideal clients or not.

As the customer/client, if you don't really need the program but feel arm-twisted into buying, chances are very good you'll end up resenting not only the program itself (and the business), but the tactics used to get you to buy. And even if you actually enjoy the program, you may still have residual icky-feelings because of how you felt when you bought.

And that's why my belief is fear WILL cost you business. Sure, in the short term you may sell more than love-based companies, but between the returns and the slow erosion of your brand as your customers end up with bad tastes in their mouths because they didn't like the way they were sold to (even if they didn't fully understand it), over time I believe love-based businesses will be more profitable.

So, in order to become a love-based business, you need to sell and market by triggering love. Remember, since buying IS an emotional experience, the only way you're going to sell is to trigger emotions. Traditional direct response copy uses both love and fear — and, in fact, most fear-based marketers will actually use both love and fear (but, remember, if they trigger any fear at all, that becomes the predominant emotion). It's like the force in Star Wars — you can use it for love or you can use it for fear. It's your choice: which emotions do you want to trigger?

I'm guessing you want to trigger love-based emotions – that's why you're here!

Now, let's talk a little bit more about what motivates people to buy.

People only buy what they want. They do NOT buy what they need.

Yes, I'll say that again — they do NOT buy what they need, only what they want. If people only bought what they needed, they would have the bare minimum of everything — clothes, food, water, shelter and heat.

But we buy what we want because we don't want just the minimum that will keep us alive. If we did, we'd all be living in tents eating ramen noodles, wrapped in blankets. But we're not. We want clothes that reflect our style; we want the type of car we prefer to drive. We want our dream house, appliances to make our life easier, electronics for fun (and maybe to make our life and business easier), organic food for our bodies, and so on.

In other words, we want an upgrade from what we actually need. And that's what we buy — the upgrade.

However, since a lot of what we're buying IS an upgrade to a need, we can still justify the purchase by saying we "need" it. The reality is, we're still just buying what we want and justifying it by saying it's what we need.

So, where does "need" come from?

As I talked about earlier in the book, our needs often stem from deep emotional and psychological survival instincts (both for ourselves and for our species) that were implanted thousands of years ago when we were living as cavemen and cavewoman and wandering the world in hunter/gather communities.

According to psychology research, we haven't changed much emotionally since living in caves and running away from saber-toothed tigers, so many of our triggers have remained the same, such as:

- Security (having enough food, a comfortable house, warm clothes, etc.)

- Attracting a mate

- Raising a family

- Taking care of our health and our emotional and spiritual well-being

- Being a part of a community (including having a role in it – serving a purpose)

The reason why those needs exist is because they're essential for our own personal survival and for the survival of our species. Making sure those needs are fulfilled is deeply buried in our subconscious. That's why, if those needs are threatened in any way, we have an almost subconscious, survival instinct reaction to the threat.

That's why if there's a problem that's keeping us up at night, chances are it can be traced back to something that's threatening (or feels like it's threatening) one of those subconscious needs. And that's why we're "triggered," because we want to make sure we protect and fulfill our needs.

For instance — we're worried about money because that's threatening our deeply embedded desire for safety, for taking care of our family, and maybe even being a part of a community. It's not that we're worried about money per se — but what money represents — our ability to take care ourselves, our family, our community, our health, etc.

And there is no question the pain is real. Whether someone is truly losing his house or is worried he's going to lose his home even though it hasn't happened yet, the pain is real. It's there, it's real, and if our mission is to help people him keep his home, then we need to address that pain and that trigger, *so we can help him.*

So then the question becomes, are we going to use the trigger in a fear-based way, or a love-based way?

Triggers that are used in a fear-based manner tend to either twist the negative emotion that's already there, or create new negative emotions.

Triggers used in a love-based manner bring up the trigger/ pain *without making it worse*. The idea is to create a buying environment where your ideal prospects firmly understand both the cost of staying in pain and the pleasure (transformation) that awaits them, so they can make a conscious choice between the two.

Now, I will be the first to admit this is a fine line, and a lot of what can make something fear-based versus love-based is the intention behind it (i.e. if you're truly committed to calling ONLY those who are ready to move forward right now, you're more likely to create copy that is love-based).

Remember, talking about the pain (and triggering the need) is simply the first step in the buying process. *Yes, you need to start with the pain or the problem, because that's where your ideal prospects are starting.* They're in real pain and are looking for a real solution.

Once they find a possible solution, they want to learn more about it — what the solution is, if it's real, if it will really help them, etc.

If their questions are answered to their satisfaction, they may take the next step and pay money for it.

So, if we go back to fear-based marketing and copy, in a lot of cases the pain is acknowledged via triggering fear-based emotions, because that will make the pain even worse.

BUT, in a lot of cases, there is then a "switch up" to love-based emotions, when describing the solution. Because what people WANT to buy is love, hope, transformation, community, respect, etc. Remember, buying is fun — if you keep going on and on about the pain, all you're going to do is turn them off.

This brings to mind a famous study where dentists were trying to figure out a way to compel kids to brush their teeth more. They divided the kids into three groups, and used three distinctly separate messages with each.

In the first group, they simply told the kids "You really should brush your teeth at least two times a day." In the second group, they said the same, but also included education about gum disease and other issues. It's important to note that they just talked about them; they didn't show any pictures. In the third group, they did all of the above, AND showed the most disgusting, horrifying pictures of what can happen when you don't brush your teeth.

So, which group do you think was the most likely to change their behavior?

Surprise - it was actually the second group. In the third group, the kids were initially horrified and said things like "Oh yes, I'm definitely going to brush my teeth more," but after a few days, their brains "buried" the horrifying images and their behavior went back to what it was before.

So what does this prove? When you go on and on about the pain, and turn it into suffering, along with dealing with all the other issues that fear-based marketing brings, you also run the risk of having your ideal clients simply "tune out" your marketing.

This is why both love and fear exist in direct response copy, because fear-based marketers used both. There really is no choice in using one without the other. Because people aren't going to buy if you only use fear. You need love in there, or it simply doesn't work.

This is also how fear-based marketers tainted love-based emotions. Again, when you mix love and fear, everything is tainted with fear. Even if you try and trigger love-based emotions with a fear-based mindset, it's going to sound more like fear.

Consider what's happened with hope.

Hope is a beautiful, love-based emotion. And yet, when I spoke to two of my colleagues who I very much respect, they both placed hope into fear-based marketing.

At first I was taken aback. Hope is love, not fear. But, then I thought about it, and I realized what was happening.

Just like when you approach pain via fear, it turns into suffering, when you approach hope via fear, it turns into false hope.

False hope typically happens when you sell a transformation that is unlikely to occur for the vast majority of folks. For instance, when someone sells the "You can make an additional $10,000 a month working an extra hour a week" concept, they're selling false hope. While yes, I'm sure you can find people out there who have been able to do that, it's not the norm and it most definitely isn't something you'll be able to package and sell.

At its worst, false hope preys on people's dreams. When I was deep in the fiction writing world, I remember the dozens and dozens of businesses set up to help writers get published. Now while a lot of those were downright scams, a significant chunk had enough truth mixed in them to be an actual business - but the success stories were few and far between.

So, when you talk about hope, make sure you don't fall into giving false hope via exaggeration, by promising miraculous transformations for *everyone* (yes even if you've witnessed miraculous transformations). When you're selling via love, it's so important to come from a place of love and abundance (not desperation), knowing that everything will work out as it should... and that *everyone* is being served at the highest level.

Now, once the solution has been explained, it's time to make an offer. If you make an offer via fear, it's probably going to sound very pushy and hype-y and sales-y. This is when fear-based marketers will typically touch on shame and guilt, especially if they feel like they're losing you. Or, they may simply try and steamroll your objections and exhaust you into saying "yes."

If that's how you view the process of making an offer, it's no wonder you want nothing to do with sales and marketing.

If you'd like to make an offer the love-based way, I'd like you to change your perspective, and consider making an offer as the opportunity to be of service to the people you're meant to serve. (My friend Lisa Sasevich often says it's a disservice to not make an offer – and I totally agree.)

You see, your ideal clients are looking for you. (In fact, I dare say they *need* you.) They are truly in pain right now, and if you don't make them an offer, they're never going to get the transformation they're looking for.

And that is a true shame.

Think of all the people you're meant to help that simply won't be helped without you.

Now, you might be thinking "But then maybe I should give it away for free."

Well, maybe. But let's consider this first:

As humans, we're drawn to live in and be an active part of a community. And, to live happily in a community, we're also wired to want "even exchanges" of energy.

You scratch my back, I'll scratch yours.

Money is simply a way to exchange energy. You give someone money in exchange for something they've put their time and energy into creating for you — whether it's a new pair of shoes or a book or a steak dinner or coaching program.

If you try and stop that flow, i.e. give what you've created away for free, what you've done is actually create an imbalance. People have your creation without compensating you in return.

And, when that happens, in a lot of cases, the people you've given your creation to don't value it.

So, they won't use it.

If you want to test this, let a few people who have expressed interest in your program in for free and watch what they do. In the vast majority of cases, what they'll do is nothing — they won't participate or even go through the information.

So, if you truly want to make the biggest impact you truly can, not only do you want to make an offer, but you should get paid when people accept it.

Above all, love DOES sell. People WANT to buy the emotions that are associated with love. Our job as business owners and entrepreneurs is to make sure we are standing in love and abundance ourselves, so when we reach out, our "come from" IS that of love and abundance.

We don't run after them when they say "no."

We don't make them feel bad when they say "no."

We don't encourage them to buy if we know in our gut they aren't a good fit.

Instead, we create the perfect buying environment for our ideal clients that respects their space for making their own decisions - and asks them honestly if they're ready to be done with their pain and experience transformation, instead. And we honor the decision they make.

In the next chapter, I cover specifics of how this looks in copy.

Chapter 7
CHOOSE LOVE-BASED TRIGGERS VERSUS FEAR-BASED TRIGGERS

Now it's time for the fun part! Let's roll up our sleeves and take a look at specific examples of how love-based triggers and fear-based triggers show up in copy.

URGENCY AS A TRIGGER:

Urgency is important because without it, there's no reason for anyone to buy now. They'll wait to buy for a better time, to have more money, etc. And in the vast majority of cases, when folks wait to buy, what ends up happening is they never buy.

That's why including urgency in your copy is so important. And urgency, in and of itself, is not the problem. The problem is fear-based copywriting tactics have misused urgency, leaving a lot of entrepreneurs with a sour taste in their mouth.

How do they misuse it? By making it fake.

Fake urgency is clearly made up urgency — like you only have 10 digital products to sell. Or you're out and out lying about why you either have a deadline or a limit on the number of products to sell.

So, the way to use urgency correctly is to not use fake urgency. Have a real, true-life reason why you're closing down enrollment or raising the price. Maybe the program is starting. Or this is the one time of year you have a sale on your product. (Stores periodically have sales with ending dates.) Or you're offering your time and there is a limit as to how many spots you're going to open.

Following are more tips on using urgency in a love-based way:

💜 Make sure you have a solid reason for doing whatever it is you're doing (closing enrollment, taking a product off the market or raising the price) — and clearly communicate that reason to your ideal prospects.

Good reasons for doing the above:

💜 The program is about to start and you want to take care of the folks who are enrolled.

💜 You're discontinuing the product (or you're upgrading it or coming out with a new version or some variation of that).

💜 You have a limited number of spots available because of the amount of time each participant is getting.

💜 It's a new product and you're offering it at an introductory price

💜 You're offering early bird pricing.

- You're having a sale — birthday sale, end-of-year sale, clean-the-closet out sale, etc.

- You can also use bonuses — either adding new bonuses or taking away existing bonuses — to encourage people to buy now. But again, there should be a reason why bonuses are being added or removed — maybe the bonus has a deadline (you're offering a special call on X date) or you're doing a final push and offering a special bonus at the every end. Or you can add a bonus that provides time with you, which has a natural limiter of only a handful who can do it since your time is limited.

- You can also use payment plans ending, but this isn't as strong as some of the other ones.

(For more ideas on having a sale or a promotion, check out my "Holiday Marketing Secrets" Kindle report, which has ideas for sales anytime of the year: LoveBasedCopyBooks.com.)

YOU CAN ALSO COMBINE PAIN AND URGENCY:

In other words, let your ideal prospects know what the cost is to not ending their pain now. What is it going to feel like when they still have the same problem 3 months, 6 months, 2 years from now? Is that what they really want their life to look like?

Again, don't be overdramatic or use shame or guilt or sound judgmental or tap into fear — it's a fair question to ask them if they fully understand the cost of not solving their pain, and you can explain the cost. It becomes fear-based when you go overboard.

The easiest way to do this in a love-based way is to simply restate the pain you touch on at the beginning. An example is below:

> Ask yourself this: Where will I be in three months time?
>
> Will you still be struggling with your marketing? Not getting the leads or clients you need to keep your business alive?

USING PLEASURE AS A TRIGGER:

In love-based copy, you want to focus on the transformation your ideal clients are looking for. People buy hope — so give them hope. Spend most of the copy on the transformation they'll receive and make it clear that YES, this transformation is open to them, as well. People just like them were able to transform — they can do it too. That's very compelling and inviting.

NOT USING EXAGGERATION AS A TRIGGER:

Okay, so this is about what not to do instead of what to do, but this is too important to not talk about.

Exaggerating and over-exaggerating is the lazy way to get people to take action — you exaggerate the pain or the fear AND you exaggerate the results or the transformation. However, when you exaggerate, you also trigger people's natural skepticism, so while you may get their initial attention, you may NOT get the desired action unless you take steps to overcome the skepticism (and no, just saying "it sounds incredible but it's true" doesn't work).

So keep it real. If you've truly tapped into what your ideal clients are looking for — what's keeping them up at night and what transformation they're looking for — there's no need to exaggerate.

"UNSELLING" AS A TRIGGER:

Unselling (or "take away" selling) is when you take the sale away. In other words, you can actually clarify who would not be right for the program. This can be a powerful way to make it clear to your ideal prospects the consequences of the choice they're making.

The way you normally see this, is something like:

> Who is right for the program? (Then, use bullets to describe who you're looking for.)
>
> Who is not right for the program? (Then, use bullets to describe who you're not looking for.)

When you see this done in a fear-based way, there tends to be a lot of shaming and making people feel "less than" because they don't measure up. If you approach this in a love-based way, you can simply clarify, without judgment, who you're looking for and let your ideal prospects sort out if they're ready to move forward with your solution or not.

Here's a fear-based example:

> Successful people make time for programs like this because they know it's going to change their life. If you don't feel like you can make the time, you're probably not ready to be successful yet.

Here's an example of how you can do this in a love-based way:

> This program is not for everyone. If you're more comfortable growing slowly and taking things one step at a time, this is not for you. And that's fine, not everyone wants to move quickly. But if you're someone who wants to go big fast and take a quantum leap in your business, then this may be exactly what you're looking for.

And lastly, if it doesn't feel good to you, don't use it. Look, it's your business and your reputation. If you don't like how something is phrased or the choice of words, then don't use it. Find another way to say it that feels good to you. (And if you're working with an independent copywriter, I encourage you to have a conversation with the copywriter. I know when I work with clients and see edits — I always look at the edits from the perspective of "Will this hurt conversions?" If I believe what the client wants to change won't make a difference in conversions, I'll leave the changes. But if I believe their changes will hurt conversions, I'll ask why they want to change it, and depending on their answer, I'll look for another way to accomplish the same goal.)

So, now that we've covered the basics of love-based copywriting, let's take a moment in the final chapter to pull it all together.

Chapter 8
PULLING IT ALL TOGETHER

Now that you understand the main principles of love-based copywriting, the last step is to help you implement these principles into your own marketing and copywriting.

As I've shared, my own feeling is there is a lot of good in direct response copywriting, and if we approach direct response copywriting from a love-based perspective, we'll be able to grow our business and make a bigger difference in the world, and feel great about how we do it.

I've shared the main ways fear can show up in copy and given you ways to replace fear with love. And if you combine that with a love-based mindset and "come from," and write to your ideal client as if you are writing to a friend, you should be well on your way to creating love-based copy.

(Want some additional help? I've put together a love-based copywriting template to make it even easier to integrate what you learned in this book into your own copy and marketing. You can download the template for free at: LoveBasedCopywritingBook.com/template.)

Depending on where you are now and where you want to go, I've also put together a collection of resources to help you on your love-based journey in the Resources section.

Lastly, remember we are stronger together than we are alone. If all of us start to implement love-based copywriting principles, we will transform the direct response copywriting industry. None of us can do it alone, but together we can have an impact.

And when that happens, imagine how wonderful it will be to know that our marketing is a force of good and love as strong as our gifts and missions are.

That's when we know we've truly made a difference!

Love and success,

Michele PW

About the Author
ABOUT MICHELE PW

Considered one of the hottest direct
response copywriters and
marketing consultants in the
industry today, Michele PW
(Michele Pariza Wacek) has a
reputation for crafting copy and
creating online and offline
marketing campaigns that get
results.

Michele started writing
professionally in 1992, working
at agencies and on staff as a marketing/communication/writing
specialist. In 1998, she started her business as a freelance
copywriter.

But she quickly realized her vision was bigger than serving
her clients as a one-woman-shop. In 2004, she began the
transformation to building a copywriting and marketing
company.

Two years later, her vision turned into reality. Michele PW/
Creative Concepts and Copywriting LLC is the premiere direct
response copywriting and marketing company today, catering
to entrepreneurs and small business owners internationally,

including the "Who's Who" of Internet Marketing. Some of their clients include:

- ❤ Ali Brown

- ❤ Lisa Sasevich

- ❤ Brian Tracy

- ❤ John Assaraf

- ❤ Bernadette Doyle

- ❤ Alex Mandossian

- ❤ Kendall SummerHawk

- ❤ Alexis Martin Neely

In addition, Michele is also a national speaker and the bestselling author of the "Love-Based Copywriting" books that teach people how to write copy that attracts, inspires and invites. She has also completed two novels.

She holds a double major in English and Communications from the University of Wisconsin-Madison. Currently she lives in the mountains of Prescott, Arizona with her husband Paul and her border collie Nick and southern squirrel hunter Cassie.

Resources

Additional Books in my Love-Based Business Series available here: http://LoveBasedPublishing.com

LOVE-BASED COPYWRITING METHOD COPMANION RESOURCE

I've put together a love-based copywriting template to help you integrate love-based principles in your copy. You can download it for free here:

LoveBasedCopywritingBook.com/template

OTHER BOOKS BY MICHELE PW

LOVE-BASED COPYWRITING SYSTEM: A STEP-BY-STEP PROCESS TO MASTER WRITING COPY THAT ATTRACTS, INSPIRES AND INVITES
(VOLUME 2 IN THE LOVE-BASED BUSINESS SERIES)

This is a copywriting course in book format. This "how to" book walks you through exactly how to write love-based copy. It includes exercises, copy templates and more. If you're planning on doing any sort of writing for your business - for instance, writing emails or website copy - this book is a must-have.

http://lovebasedpublishing.com/lbs/copywriting-system

93

LOVE-BASED ONLINE MARKETING: CAMPAIGNS TO GROW A BUSINESS YOU LOVE AND THAT LOVES YOU BACK

(VOLUME 3 IN THE LOVE-BASED BUSINESS SERIES)

All successful, profitable businesses need a marketing plan, and this book walks you through how to create a specific online marketing plan perfect for you. You'll also learn the basics about how to sell products and services online without feeling sales-y, and what might be standing in your way of successfully marketing your business.

http://lovebasedpublishing.com/lbs/online-marketing

LOVE-BASED MONEY AND MINDSET: MAKE THE MONEY YOU DESIRE WITHOUT SELLING YOUR SOUL

(VOLUME 4 IN THE LOVE-BASED BUSINESS SERIES)

For many of us, money is a source of angst. Love-Based Money and Mindset is designed to help you heal your relationship with money so you not only feel peaceful about it, but so you're also able to attract all the abundance you want. While this book is designed to help everyone who struggles with money issues, it's particularly helpful for those who have (or want to have) a business.

The bottom line: The more you can cultivate a love-based mindset, the more easily and effortlessly you'll attract money into your life.

http://lovebasedpublishing.com/lbs/money-mindset

HOW TO START A BUSINESS YOU LOVE AND THAT LOVES YOU BACK: GET CLEAR ON YOUR PURPOSE & PASSION - BUILD A SUCCESSFUL, PROFITABLE BUSINESS

PART OF THE LOVE-BASED BUSINESS SERIES

This book includes exercises and questions to ask yourself to make sure the heart of your business reflects what you really want it to. It's about answering the deeper questions around your business, like why you want it in the first place - because the more clear you are in your answers to those questions, the more satisfied you'll most likely be with what you eventually build.

I wrote this book for you if you don't have a business yet, but you want to get started, and you're intrigued by the idea of having a business you love and that loves you back.

http://lovebasedpublishing.com/lbs/start-a-biz

95

OTHER KINDLE BOOKS BY MICHELE PW

"The Dirty Little Secret About Direct Response/ Internet Marketing: Why What You've Been Taught Isn't Working for You and What You Can Do to Turn it Around" — LoveBasedCopyBooks.com

"5 Mistakes Entrepreneurs and Small Business Owners Make When They Hire a Copywriter and How to Avoid Them. PLUS 10 Questions You Should Ask/Tasks You Should Do BEFORE You Hire a Copywriter" — LoveBasedCopyBooks.com

"Holiday Marketing Secrets — How to Grow Your Biz Year-Round (And yes, these strategies can help you build a more successful and profitable biz no matter what time of year it is)" — LoveBasedCopyBooks.com

"LOVE-BASED MARKETING"

Book by Susan Liddy — "Love-Based Marketing: The No Sell-Out, Copy-Out, Burn-Out Method to Attract Your Soul Mate Clients into Your Business" www.SusanLiddy.com

Don't want to write your own copy but still want it love-based?

We would be happy to write your copy for you! See the next page for details.

DONE-FOR-YOU COPYWRITING SERVICES — GET MORE LEADS, CLIENTS AND SALES WITHOUT DOING THE WORK YOURSELF!

As a busy entrepreneur or small business owner, you're probably looking for ways to leverage your time and money. Well, there's no better leverage than direct response copywriting.

Consider this — copywriting leverages your marketing and your selling. You can make money without picking up the phone and selling one-on-one. (Imagine the time saving right there.) You can easily add multiple streams of income to your business. You can turn your website into a lead-generation tool so you have a consistently full pipeline of clients. You can send out an email or a direct mail piece and watch money flow into your business!

That's the beauty of direct response copywriting.

But there's only one small problem — if you want results, you need to be trained. And, as a busy entrepreneur or small business owner, who has time for training?

That's why I'd like to introduce you to the Michele PW Done-For-You Copywriting Services. Whether you're looking for a one-shot copy project (like getting your website written or a few emails or a postcard) or an entire project launch campaign, or a combination of copywriting and marketing strategy, our team of trained copywriters and marketing strategists can take care of your needs and (even more importantly) get you the results you're looking for.

WANT TO LEARN MORE? JUST EMAIL OR CALL FOR THE DETAILS — INFO@MICHELEPW.COM OR (TOLL FREE) 877-754-3384 X2.

(Note — we also write articles, press releases, social networking posts and more.

Just ask if you want to learn more.)

TESTIMONIALS

"Working with Michele PW was such a relief because she GETS direct response copywriting. She knew what I was looking for and was able to deliver. With her help, we had record-breaking numbers for one of our campaigns. I highly recommend Michele if you're looking for copywriting that gets you results."

Ali Brown
Founder of Alexandria Brown International
www.AlexandriaBrown.com

"With Michele's copywriting and social networking help, I had my BIGGEST 6-figure launch ever! And I'm no stranger to 6-figure product launches. Before Michele, I had 5 6-figure launches. But this one I did with Michele blew all the other ones away. We more than doubled what I had done before. Plus, even though I knew the launch was on track, there were moments I panicked because I wasn't staying up until 2 a.m. writing copy. I highly recommend Michele, especially if you're getting ready to launch a new product or service."

Lisa Sasevich
The Queen of Sales Conversion
www.LisaSasevich.com

"I've had the pleasure of working with some of the top marketing minds of our time, and as far as results are concerned, Michele is right there with them. One idea she gave me for one of my recent launches, directly resulted in a 30% increase of sales. I'm planning on implementing that idea on a regular basis the results were so powerful. Thanks Michele!"

Mark Harris
Co-Founder www.ThoughtLeaderSecrets.com

"With Michele's expert copywriting and marketing help, we're averaging an 8% conversion rate! Considering that 1% is typically considered really good by industry standards, we were blown away by the results."

Linda H. Hunt
Owner
www.sumsolutions.com

"Thanks to your eagle eye and copywriting changes to ONE simple email I increased registrations for my "Give Your Pricing a Kick-in-the-Pants" Virtual Workshop Intensive by 20%! That's money that went straight into my bank account!"

Kendall SummerHawk
The "Horse Whisperer for Business"
Author, "How to Charge What You're Worth and Get It!"
www.KendallSummerHawk.com

Made in the USA
Lexington, KY
10 November 2019

56824721R00063